Key Stage 2 LEARN
Shape, Size & Distance

NAPE
National Association for Primary Education

Contents

AUTHOR: Camilla de la Bédoyère
EDITORIAL: Catherine de la Bédoyère, Quentin de la Bédoyère, John Bolt, Vicky Garrard, Kate Lawson, Sally MacGill, Julia Rolf, Lyndall Willis
DESIGN: Jen Bishop, Dave Jones, Colin Rudderham
ILLUSTRATORS: David Benham, Sarah Wimperis
PRODUCTION: Chris Herbert, Claire Walker
Thanks also to Robert Walster

COMMISSIONING EDITOR: Polly Willis
PUBLISHER AND CREATIVE DIRECTOR: Nick Wells

3 book Pack ISBN 1-84451-053-0   Book ISBN 1-84451-031-X
6 book Pack ISBN 1-84451-066-2   Book ISBN 1-84451-082-4
First published in 2003

A copy of the CIP data for this book is available from the British Library upon request.

Created and produced by
FLAME TREE PUBLISHING
Crabtree Hall,
Crabtree Lane,
Fulham, London SW6 6TY
United Kingdom
www.flametreepublishing.com

Flame Tree Publishing is part of The Foundry Creative Media Co. Ltd.

© The Foundry Creative Media Co. Ltd, 2003

Printed in Croatia

Foreword

Sometimes when I am crossing the playground on my way to visit a primary school I pass young children playing at schools. There is always a stern authoritarian little teacher at the front laying down the law to the unruly group of children in the pretend class. This puzzles me a little because the school I am visiting is very far from being like the children's play. Where do they get this Victorian view of what school is like? Perhaps it's handed down from generation to generation through the genes. Certainly they don't get it from their primary school. Teachers today are more often found alongside their pupils, who are learning by actually doing things for themselves, rather than merely listening and obeying instructions.

Busy children, interested and involved in their classroom reflect what we know about how they learn. Of course they learn from teachers but most of all they learn from their experience of life and their life is spent both in and out of school. Indeed, if we compare the impact upon children of even the finest schools and teachers, we find that three or four times as great an impact is made by the reality of children's lives outside the school. That reality has the parent at the all important centre. No adult can have so much impact, for good or ill, as the young child's mother or father.

This book, and others in the series, are founded on the sure belief that the great majority of parents want to help their children grow and learn and that teachers are keen to support them. The days when parents were kept at arm's length from schools are long gone and over the years we have moved well beyond the white line painted on the playground across which no parent must pass without an appointment. Now parents move freely in and out of schools and very often are found in the classrooms backing up the teachers. Both sides of the partnership know how important it is that children should be challenged and stimulated both in and out of school.

Perhaps the most vital part of this book is where parents and children are encouraged to develop activities beyond those offered on the page. The more the children explore and use the ideas and techniques we want them to learn, the more they will make new knowledge of their very own. It's not just getting the right answer, it's growing as a person through gaining skill in action and not only in books. The best way to learn is to live.

I remember reading a story to a group of nine year old boys. The story was about soldiers and of course the boys, bloodthirsty as ever, were hanging on my every word. I came to the word khaki and I asked the group "What colour is khaki?" One boy was quick to answer. "Silver" he said, "It's silver." "Silver? I queried. "Yes," he said with absolute confidence, "silver, my Dad's car key is silver." Now I reckon I'm a pretty good teller of stories to children but when it came down to it, all my dramatic reading of a gripping story gave way immediately to the power of the boy's experience of life. That meant so much more to him, as it does to all children.

JOHN COE
General Secretary
National Association for Primary Education (NAPE).

NAPE was founded 23 years ago with the aim of improving the quality of teaching and learning in primary schools. The association brings together parents and teachers in partnership.

NAPE, Moulton College, Moulton, Northampton, NN3 7RR, Telephone: 01604 647 646 Web: www. nape.org.uk

Shape, Size and Distance is one of six books in the **Learn** series, which has been devised to help you support your child through Key Stage Two.

The National Curriculum gives teachers clear guidelines on what subjects should be studied in Mathematics, and to what level. These guidelines have been used to form the content of both this book and **Addition, Subtraction, Multiplication & Division**, the accompanying maths text in this series.

Each page contains exercises for your child to complete, an activity they can complete away from the book and **Parents Start Here** boxes to give you extra information and guidance. At the end of the book you will find a checklist of topics – you can use this to mark off each topic as it is mastered.

This book has been designed for children to work through alone; but it is recommended that you read the book first to acquaint yourself with the material it contains. Try to be at hand when your child is working with the book; your input is valuable. The teaching of mathematics has changed since you were at school and you may find you can learn something useful too!

Encourage good study habits in your child:

Try to set aside a short time every day for studying. 10 to 20 minutes a day is plenty. Start each learning session with two minutes spent on mental maths; your child will be used to doing this at school.

- Establish a quiet and comfortable environment for your child to work and provide suitable equipment. Your child will need sharp pencils, a ruler, rubber, scrap paper, graph paper and protractor to complete this book.

- Give your child access to drinking water whenever they work; research suggests this helps them perform better.

- Reward your child; plenty of praise for good work motivates children to succeed.

- Ensure your child eats a healthy diet, gets plenty of rest and lots of opportunity to play.

This book is intended to support your child in their school work. Sometimes children find particular topics hard to understand; discuss this with their teacher, who may be able to suggest alternative ways to help your child.

For this book, your child will need to have some or all of the following equipment:

Protractor   Graph paper   Tracing paper   Ruler

Pencil   Rubber   Paper clips   A pin   Glue

Parents Start Here...

Top Tip!
Bring what your child learns into everyday life – they'll remember it even better.

In just a few pages' time you are going to need a protractor – so make sure you have one in the house and it might be an idea to just remind yourself how to measure angles with it.

Angles

Stand up and face the door. Keep your feet on the same spot but swivel round so you are facing the window. The amount you have just turned is called an angle. You can sit down now.

- An angle is a measure of turn.
- We measure angles in degrees and we use this symbol: °

If you face the door, then turn all the way round until you are facing the door again, you have turned 360°.

Stand up again and turn 360°.

Now turn 180°. Here is a clue: 180 is half of 360.

Look at these lines:

Imagine we could swivel line A so that it was lying on top of Line B. The amount we had to swivel, or turn, Line A is called an angle.

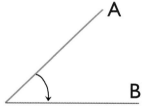

This angle measures 90° and it is called a right angle.

We use this symbol to show it is a right angle.

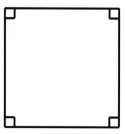

Right angles are important because all of the corners in squares and rectangles are right angles.

An angle that measures less than 90° is called an acute angle.
We use this symbol to show that it is not a right angle.

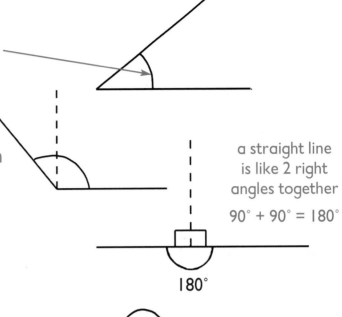

An angle that measures more than 90° is called an obtuse angle.

a straight line is like 2 right angles together

90° + 90° = 180°

A straight line measures 180°.

180°

An angle that measures more than 180° is called a reflex angle.

Home Learn

Put an o next to the obtuse angles, r next to the right angles and a next to the acute angles.

Activity

Look at your hands and find the angles between your thumbs and forefingers. Move your thumbs to make right angles and acute angles. Can you stretch to make an obtuse angle?

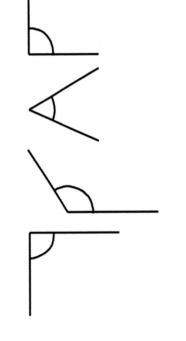

Check Your Progress!

Angles

Turn to page 48 and put a tick next to what you have just learned.

Parents Start Here...

Children are expected to know all of the terms used on this page, and they should be able to draw simple 2-D shapes and patterns.

2-D Shapes

- A 2-D shape is flat. The name comes from the word dimensions. The two dimensions are length and width.
- 2-D shapes are also called plane shapes.
- 2-D shapes with 3 sides are called triangles.
- 2-D shapes with 4 sides are called quadrilaterals.
- 2-D shapes with straight sides are also called polygons.

Square

A square has 4 sides that are all the same length. It has 4 right angles.

Rectangle

A rectangle has two pairs of equal sides and 4 right angles.

Rhombus

A rhombus has 4 sides of equal length but no right angles. The opposite sides are parallel.

Parallelogram

A parallelogram has two pairs of equal sides but no right angles.

Trapezium

A trapezium has 1 pair of parallel sides.

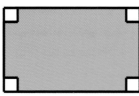

Kite

A kite has 2 pairs of equal length sides that are next to one another. There are no parallel sides.

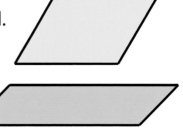

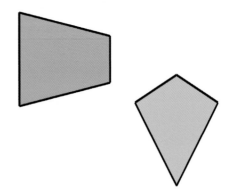

Pentagon
A pentagon has 5 sides.

Hexagon
A hexagon has 6 sides.

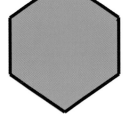

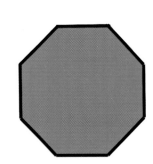

Heptagon
A heptagon has 7 sides.

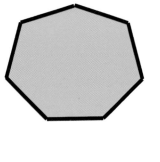

Octagon
An octagon has 8 sides.

Parallel lines run side by side forever, never touching one another.

Home Learn

Complete these sentences:
a) A quadrilateral has _____ sides.
b) A triangle has _____ sides.
c) A pentagon has _____ sides.
d) A hexagon has _____ sides.
e) An octagon has _____ sides.

Activity

Practise drawing the shapes on this page. You might find a tracing paper or graph paper useful and you will need a ruler to draw straight lines.

Check Your Progress!

2-D Shapes

Turn to page 48 and put a tick next to what you have just learned.

Top Tip!
Go through this page as often as you like until your child understands it fully.

Parents Start Here...

Since 3-D shapes are difficult to visualise, especially from pictures in a book, support this topic with a look at solid objects at home.

3-D Shapes

- 3-D shapes are solid, not flat.
- 3-D shapes have height, width and depth.
- 3-D shapes can have corners, edges and faces.
- 3-D shapes that have rectangular faces and 2 identical and parallel end faces are called prisms.
- 3-D shapes with triangular faces that meet at a point are called pyramids.

edge

corner

height

face

depth

width

Cube

Cuboid

Triangular prism

Cylinder

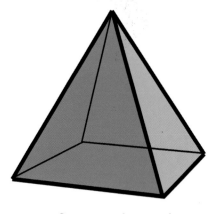

Square based
pyramid

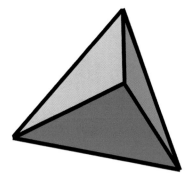

Regular
tetrahedron

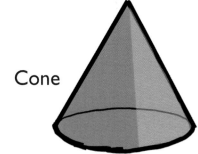

Cone

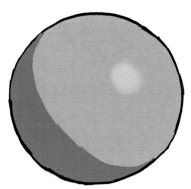

Sphere

Home Learn

Complete this table:

3-D Shape	Corners	Edges	Faces
cube	8		6
cuboid		12	
triangular prism	6		5
square based pyramid		8	
regular tetrahedron	4		4

Activity

Find objects at home that are the same as the 3-D shapes shown here.

Check Your Progress!

3-D Shapes

Turn to page 48 and put a tick next to what you have just learned.

Parents Start Here...

Help your child complete the activity; if they start with a right angle the activity will be easier.

Triangles

We have learned that triangles are polygons with 3 straight sides.

There are 4 different types of triangle, and they all have different names which you will need to learn.

An equilateral triangle has 3 sides that are all the same length.
The angles are all the same too.

A right-angled triangle has one angle that is a right angle.

An isosceles triangle has 2 sides the same length, and 2 equal angles.

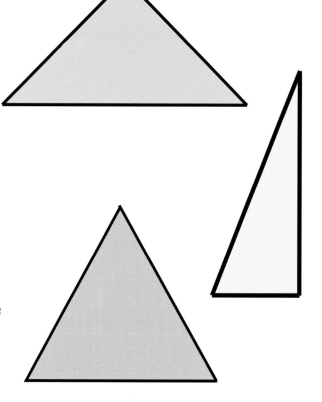

A scalene triangle has no equal angles and no equal sides.

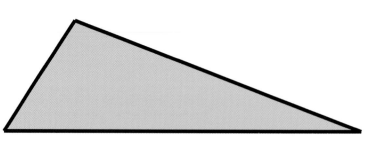

Measuring Angles

This is a protractor and it is used for measuring angles. You need to have one.

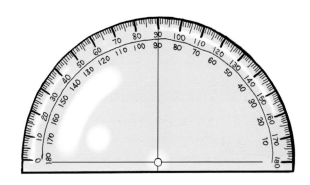

Look at this angle.
Can you tell whether it is more or less than 90°?

Now use your protractor to help you measure it.

lay the protractor along the line
read the measurement here

Was your original estimate correct?

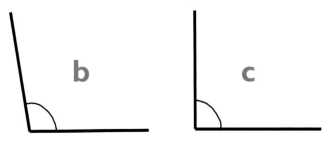

Home Learn

Use your protractor to measure these angles:

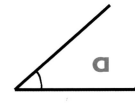

a   b   c

TRY THIS Activity

Draw any triangle you like on graph paper and then measure the angles. If you add up all the angles they should total 180°.

Check Your Progress!

Triangles

Turn to page 48 and put a tick next to what you have just learned.

Parents Start Here...

Help your child measure the perimeter of their bedroom.

Measuring Perimeters

The perimeter of a shape is the distance all the way round its sides.

Betty decides to walk all the way round her garden which is a rectangular shape.

Betty wants to find out how far she has walked. How can she do that?

The obvious way to do it is to add up all the distances Betty walked:
20 m + 10 m + 20 m + 10 m = 60 m

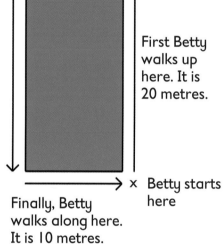

Then Betty walks along here. It is 10 metres.

Then Betty walks down here. It is 20 metres.

First Betty walks up here. It is 20 metres.

Finally, Betty walks along here. It is 10 metres.

x Betty starts here

Betty has worked out the perimeter of her garden and found it to be 60 m.

> To find the perimeter of a shape add up the lengths of all the sides.

This shape does not have the measurements of the lengths written in. How can you work out the perimeter? Easy – get out your ruler and measure it yourself!

Perimeter = _____ cm + _____ cm + _____ cm + _____ cm = _____ cm

Look at this shape. Not all of the measurements have been given to you. Do you have enough information to work out the measurements for (a) and (b)?

(a) = 10 m − 3 m = 7 m
(b) = 11 m − 8 m = 3 m

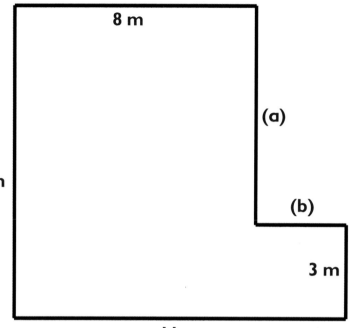

not actual size

Now you can add all of the measurements:
Perimeter = 3 m + 11 m + 10 m + 8 m + 7 m + 3 m = 42 m

Home Learn

Work out the perimeter of this shape:

Activity

Draw some rectangles and squares of your own and practise working out their perimeters.

Check Your Progress!
Measuring Perimeters
Turn to page 48 and put a tick next to what you have just learned.

13

Parents Start Here...

Assist your child as they conduct the above experiment in creating two triangles out of a rectangle. You can help your child discover the formula for calculating the area of a triangle.

Top Tip! Don't worry if your child does not understand straightaway – children learn at different speeds.

Measuring Area

The area of a flat shape is how much surface it takes up.
You can measure area in two ways:

Method One: You can measure the area of some shapes by counting the squares. There are 10 squares in this rectangle, and each square measures 1 centimetre.

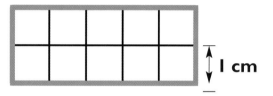

1 cm

We say that the rectangle is 10 square centimetres.

We write it like this: 10 cm^2

Method Two: Multiply the width by the length.

If you look again at the rectangle above you will see that there are 5 squares along the top, and 2 squares down. If you had done this multiplication, you would have reached the same answer: $5 \times 2 = 10$

This method works with rectangles and squares.

Complete the third example yourself.

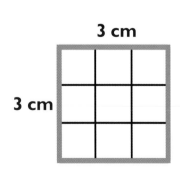

3 cm

3 cm

$3\text{cm} \times 3\text{cm} = 9\text{cm}^2$

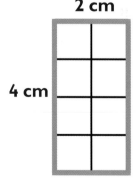

2 cm

4 cm

$4 \text{ cm} \times 2\text{cm} = 8\text{cm}^2$

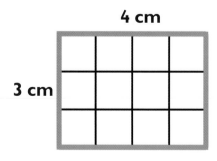

4 cm

3 cm

___ x ___ = ___ cm²

If you have a shape that is not a simple square or rectangle, or does not have any squares to count, you can still work out the area.

Look at this shape. The best way to work out the area is to imagine cutting it into two easier shapes.

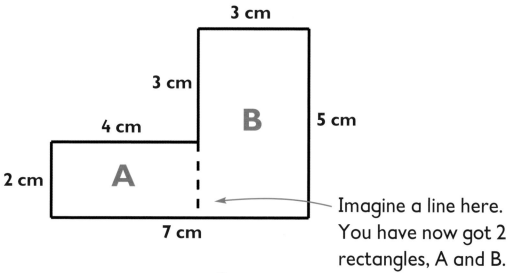

Imagine a line here. You have now got 2 rectangles, A and B.

the area of A = 4 m x 2 m = 8 m^2
the area of B = 3 m x 5 m = 15 m^2
Add the two areas to get the overall total: 8 m^2 + 15 m^2 = 23 m^2

Home Learn

Work out the area of this shape:

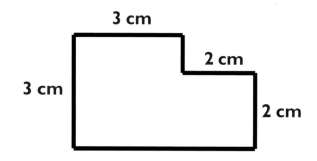

 ## Activity

Cut a rectangle in two, from corner to corner. You will find you have 2 identical triangles. The way to measure the area of a triangle is to multiply its width by its height, then halve your answer. Try this for yourself.

Check Your Progress!
Measuring Area
Turn to page 48 and put a tick next to what you have just learned.

Top Tip! Learning is fun, so if your child is tired, let them come back to this when they are fresh.

Parents Start Here...

Measuring with string is a technique that can be used on irregular shapes too. Help your child explore this technique.

Circles

A circle is a 2-D or plane shape. Unlike the other 2-D shapes we looked at, it does not have any straight sides or angles.

There are words to do with circles that you need to learn.

- If you draw a line right across the middle of a circle you have drawn the diameter.

Measure the diameter of this circle and write the answer here:

_____ cm.

diameter

- If you draw a line from the middle of the circle to the outer edge of a circle you have drawn the radius.

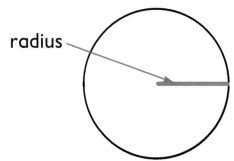

radius

The diameter of a circle is always double the radius.

Work this out:

The circus ring had a diameter of 26 m.

What was its radius? _____ m.

- The line going around the outside of a circle is called the circumference. A circumference is a circle's perimeter.

You cannot measure a circumference with a ruler because a ruler won't bend around the curvy edge. You could place a piece of string or thread around the edge, then measure the string instead.

- The circumference of a circle is always about three times its diameter.

circumference ————→

Home Learn

The diameter of a circular rug is 100 cm.

a) Estimate the rug's circumference: _____ cm

b) What is the rug's radius? _____ cm

Activity

Think of as many words as you can that start with the prefix 'circ—' Look in a dictionary to get some ideas.

Check Your Progress!

Circles

Turn to page 48 and put a tick next to what you have just learned.

Activities

1. Mark each shape with its right angles. One right angle has been put in for you.

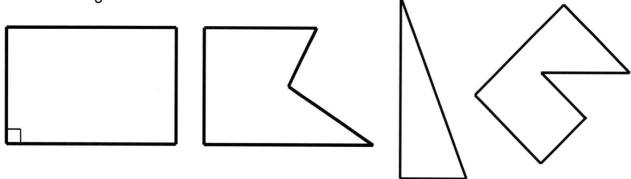

2. Draw a line from each triangle to its name. One has been drawn for you:

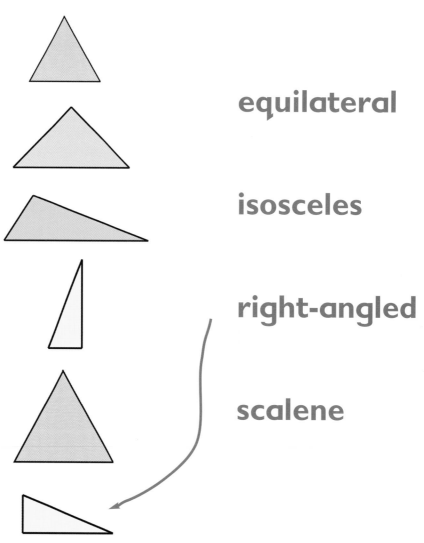

equilateral

isosceles

right-angled

scalene

3. Follow the maze to help the 3-D shape find its name.

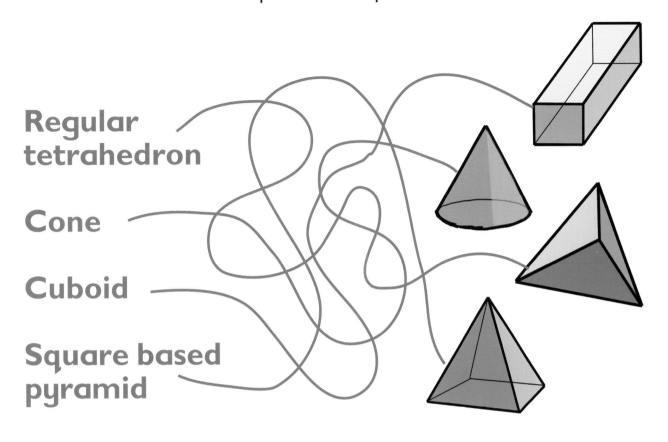

Regular
tetrahedron

Cone

Cuboid

Square based
pyramid

4. Find the area of the following triangles:

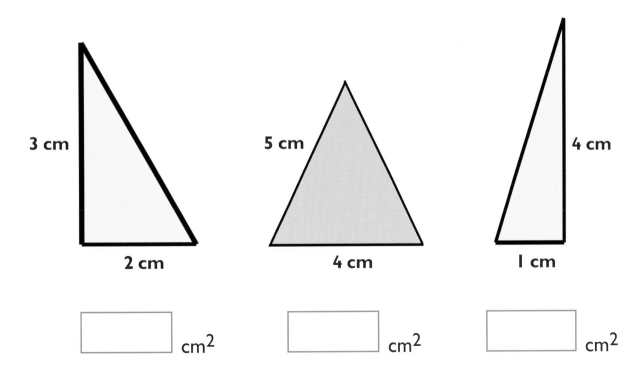

3 cm

2 cm

5 cm

4 cm

4 cm

1 cm

[ ] cm²   [ ] cm²   [ ] cm²

Parents Start Here...

Top Tip! If your child struggles with anything, don't worry – let them go at their own pace.

You will need paper (ideally graph paper), tracing paper, scissors, glue, paper clips, a pin, pencils and a ruler before your child embarks on the next few pages.

Symmetry

There are three types of symmetry you need to learn about:

• **Line Symmetry**
You may know this as reflective symmetry or mirror image.

If a shape has a line of symmetry then you can place a mirror along the line and the reflection makes the shape look unchanged:

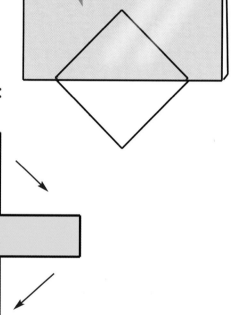

mirror

• **Rotation Symmetry**
This means turning a shape so that it looks the same.

You can turn this shape into 4 different positions and it will look the same.

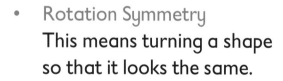

• **Translation Symmetry**
This means you can slide a shape from one place to another.
The shape does not change.

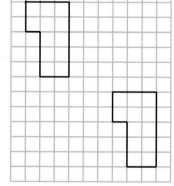

A 2-D shape may have more than one line of symmetry.
3-D shapes may have planes of symmetry rather than lines.

2-D Shapes

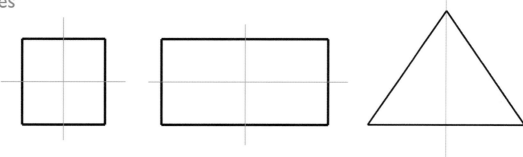

3-D Shapes

The cone has lots and lots of planes of symmetry – too many to draw in.
Can you imagine them?

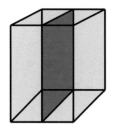
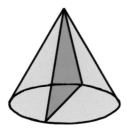

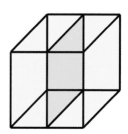

Home Learn

Draw lines of symmetry on to
these shapes:

Activity

Use scrap paper to draw some
regular polygons then cut them
out carefully. Try folding them
to find their lines of symmetry.

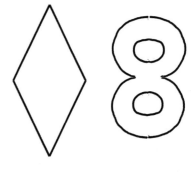

Check Your Progress!

Symmetry ☐

Turn to page 48 and put a tick next to what you have just learned.

Practise Symmetry

1. Rotational Symmetry
Trace these shapes
carefully and ask a
grown-up to help you
cut them out.

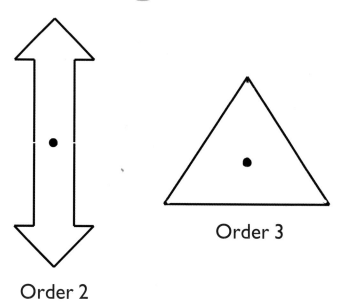

Order 2

Order 3

Place your cut-outs over the shapes and put a pin through them,
into the dots. Now turn your shape and see how many times it lines
up with the printed shape.

Shape (a) can be lined up twice. We say it has rotational symmetry
of order 2.

Shape (b) can be lined up three times. We say it has rotational
symmetry of order 3.

2. Mirror Images
Copy this shape so that it
has a mirror image. It has
been started off for you.
You could trace it if you
get stuck.

line of symmetry

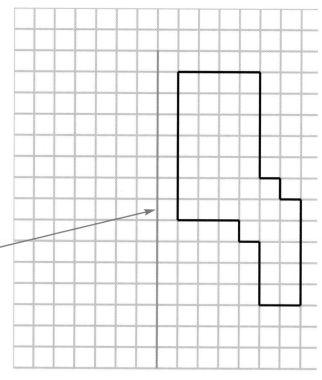

3. Translational Symmetry
Trace this shape carefully. Use a ruler to get straight lines. Cut out the shape.

Now place your cut-out on the squared grid, 2 squares along. A dot shows you where to put the corner. You have translated the shape.

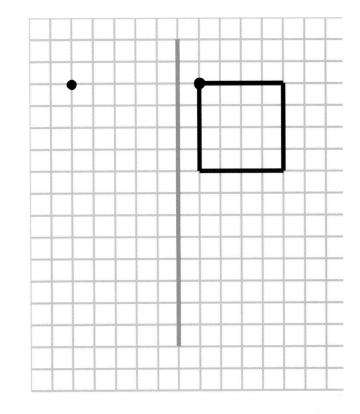

4. Finish these shapes using their lines of symmetry.
You could use a mirror or tracing paper to help you.

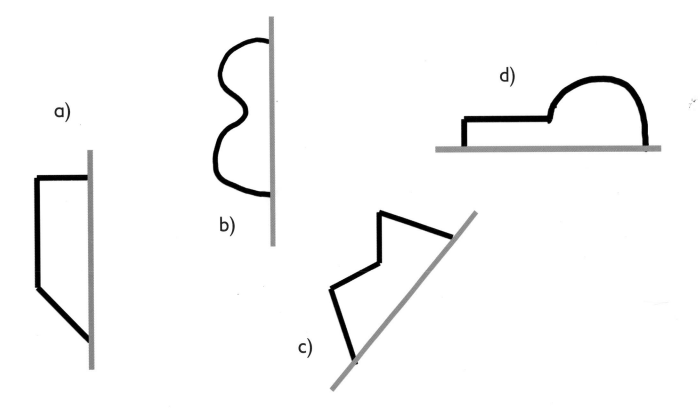

a)

b)

c)

d)

Top Tip!
Bring what your child learns into everyday life — they'll remember it even better.

Parents Start Here...

Test your child's understanding of the three dimensions by asking them to show you on solid objects around the house e.g. television, book, door.

Making 3-D Shapes

If you could take a cereal box apart, you would find that it ends up as a flat piece of cardboard. (If a grown-up actually lets you do this, it would be a good way of learning about 3-D shapes.)

You can make your own 3-D shapes by cutting and gluing card or paper. The cut-outs are called shape nets.

Here is the shape net for a cube:

Ask a grown-up to help you make the cube. Do not try to do the cutting on your own; it can be quite fiddly. Use paperclips to hold the cube in place while the glue dries.

Here is a shape net for a triangular prism. Try to make this shape too.

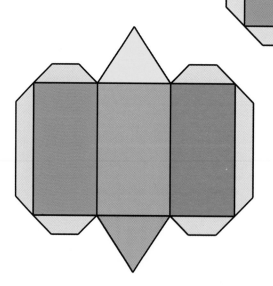

24

Working Out The Volume Of A 3-D Shape

On pages 12–15 we learned how to work out the perimeter and area of a 2-D shape. Now we need to learn how to work out the volume of a 3-D shape.

The volume of a shape is a measure of how much space that shape takes up.

We learned that 3-D shapes have 3 measurements (or dimensions). They are height, width and depth. We need to know these three measurements to work out volume:

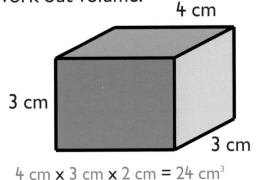

4 cm

3 cm

3 cm

4 cm x 3 cm x 2 cm = 24 cm³

It is that simple – just multiply the three measurements! When you have got your answer you must put in the symbol ³. We say 'cubed'. So we say the answer is 24 centimetres cubed.

Remember:

*   When you measure area of a 2-D shape you multiply 2 measurements, so you write the symbol ² after your answer.
*   When you measure a 3-D shape you multiply 3 measurements, so you write the symbol ³ after your answer.

Home Learn

Work out the volume of this cuboid:

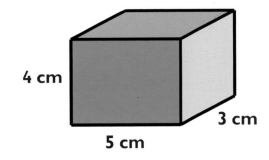

4 cm

3 cm

5 cm

Activity

Measure the three dimensions of a cereal box to the nearest centimetre, and work out the volume of the box.

Check Your Progress!
Making 3-D Shapes

Turn to page 48 and put a tick next to what you have just learned.

Top Tip!
If your child loses concentration here, let them take a break.

Parents Start Here...

Once your child is proficient at telling the time using analogue clocks you can start testing their ability to translate the time to the 24 hour clock.

Time

You probably know how to tell the time but, here are a few reminders.

Analogue Clocks

Analogue clocks have faces, or dials.

- The 12 numbers around a clock face indicate hours.
- It takes one hour, or 60 minutes, for the big hand to travel all the way around the dial, and for the little hand to move from one number to the next.
- Minutes are sometimes marked by little dots or dashes around the clock face. There are 5 minutes between each number on the face.
- The big hand points to the minutes.
- The little hand points to the hours.
- If the time is between midnight and midday (12 o'clock or noon) you say a.m.
- If the time is between midday and midnight you say p.m.

When you tell the time you need to:
- Work out what the hour is.
- Find how many minutes have passed since the o'clock.

The little hand is between the 2 and the 3 so the time is 2 hours and some minutes, or 2-something.
The big hand is pointing at 8. You can count in groups of 5 from the top of the clock (or say 8 x 5 = 40) and you will know that it is 40 minutes after 2 o'clock.
The time is 2.40 (or you can say 'twenty to three' because there are twenty minutes left before the time is 3 o'clock).

Digital Clocks

There are 24 hours in one day. Usually, we count from 1 to 12, then we start all over again. Clocks with faces can not tell you whether the time is morning, or night.

Digital clocks use the 24-hour clock. The hours are counted from 1 to 24, rather than from 1 to 12.

A digital clock looks like this:

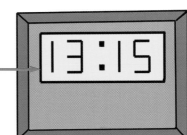

After 12 o'clock midday a digital clock shows the hours as 13, 14, 15 etc. So 13:15 is the same as 1.15 p.m.

When you write time using the 24-hour clock you must write 4 numbers:

9 o'clock in the morning is 09:00

9 o'clock in the evening is 21:00

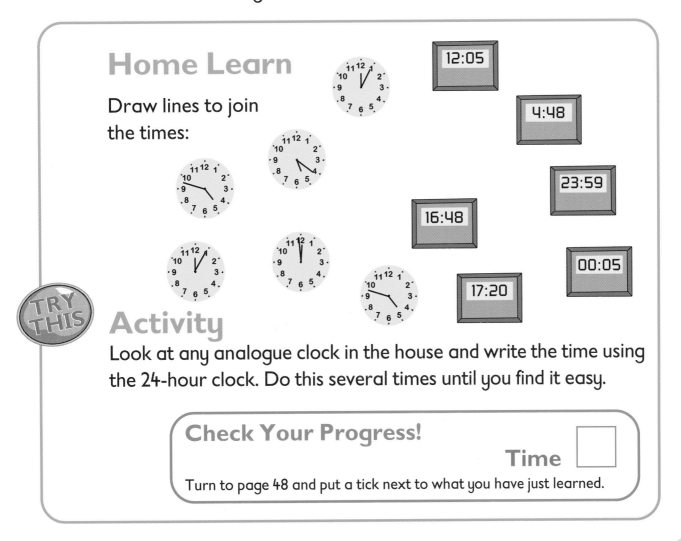

Home Learn

Draw lines to join the times:

Activity

Look at any analogue clock in the house and write the time using the 24-hour clock. Do this several times until you find it easy.

Check Your Progress!

Time

Turn to page 48 and put a tick next to what you have just learned.

Parents Start Here...

If your child has just started telling the time then do not attempt the subject of timetables yet – wait until your child is confident with time.

Adding And Subtracting Time

Arnold sets off to school at 7.35 a.m. but he arrives late at 9.05 a.m. How long does it take Arnold to get to school?

You need to work out the difference between 9.05 and 7.35 – BUT you cannot do a simple subtraction because there are 60 minutes in every hour.

Simple subtractions and additions do not work when you calculate time.

The only way to work this problem out is to keep adding on chunks of time until you get to the right answer:

Step One

7.35 |————————————————————————————| 9.05

write down the two times that you know at opposite ends of a line

Step Two

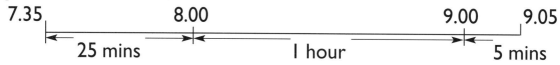

7.35   8.00   9.00   9.05

25 mins   1 hour   5 mins

Then you can add up all the times. Start with the hours:

1 hour + 25 minutes + 5 minutes = 1 hour 30 minutes

Arnold's school begins at 8.50 a.m. Can you work out what time he should leave home tomorrow in order to arrive on time?

We can work it out like this:

1. Find out how many minutes late Arnold was.
   The difference between 8.50 and 9.05 is 15 minutes.
2. Take 15 minutes off the time Arnold left for school.
   Arnold left at 7.35 a.m. Take 5 minutes off (7.30 a.m.) and then 10 minutes = 7.20 a.m.

Reading Timetables

The next time you go to a railway station take a long look at the timetables.

Timetables are very useful because they tell you what time a train leaves your station and arrives at the one you want to go to. They also show you all the other stations your train will stop at on the way, and at what times.

The problem with all this information is that it can make a train timetable look like big boxes full of numbers. Look at this bit of a train timetable:

The timetable shows the times using the 24 hour clock.

The names along the side are the names of the stations on that route. The trains are all starting at Waterloo and going to Wimbledon. The first train stops at three stations in between.

	Train A	Train B	Train C
Waterloo	14:01	14:06	14:15
Vauxhall	14:06	14:11	-
Clapham Junction	14:15	14:20	14:25
Earlsfield	14:20	-	-
Wimbledon	14:27	14:30	14:35

Home Learn

Use the timetable on this page to answer the following questions:

1. Which train does not stop at Vauxhall? _____ .

2. Eddie's Mum drops him at Clapham Junction at 14:16. Which is the first train he can catch to Wimbledon? _____ .

3. How long does it take Train A to travel from Waterloo to Wimbledon? _____ .

Activity

Ask a grown-up to help you draw a timetable for your week at school. Put in all your regular lessons and events, like assembly, breaks and after-school clubs.

Check Your Progress!
Adding And Subtracting Time

Turn to page 48 and put a tick next to what you have just learned.

Parents Start Here...

Let your child help you shop and cook.
You will both be estimating and measuring weight.

Measurements

When we learned about time we talked about hours and minutes.

These are units of time.

When we talked about perimeters and lengths we talked about centimetres and metres. These are units of length.

When we talk about measurements we need to say what the unit is.

We use metric units nowadays:

measures distance
- Millimetres (mm):   10 in a centimetre   1000 in a metre
- Centimetres (cm) :   100 in a metre
- Metres (m):   1000 in a kilometre

measures mass
- Grams (g):   1000 in a kilogram
- Kilograms (kg):   1000 in a tonne

measures volume
- Millilitres (ml)   1000 in a litre
- Litres (l)

Mass is another word for weight or how heavy something is.
Volume is a word for how much space a liquid takes up.

Imperial Measurements

You have probably heard grown-ups talking about measurements using words like inches, feet, pounds, stones, ounces, pints and miles. These are imperial measurements and grown-ups are very fond of them. The problem with imperial measurements is that they are hard to do sums with.

For example, there are:

12 inches in a foot

16 ounces in a pound

14 pounds in a stone

It all gets quite confusing. Ask your Mum how much you weighed when you were born and she'll probably give you the answer in pounds, not kilograms.

Home Learn

Complete these sentences using the correct units.

km cm g m

a) A pen is about 15 _____ long.

b) An apple weighs about 100 _____ .

c) Most people are less than 2 _____ tall.

d) I can walk 6 _____ in one hour.

Activity

The next time you are in car ask the driver to show you the counter on the dashboard that counts how many kilometres you have travelled.

Check Your Progress!
Measurements

Turn to page 48 and put a tick next to what you have just learned.

Parents Start Here...

By the end of Key Stage Two your child will need to make a rough conversion from imperial to metric units.

Scales

When we measure units we use a scale.

- A scale can be as simple as the numbers on a ruler or a measuring jug. Horses are measured in the simplest of scales – hands!

- When you use a scale you must know which units you are measuring in e.g. cm, ml.

- Using a scale is rather like using a number line – you can add and subtract along them the same way.

These are scales we use all the time:

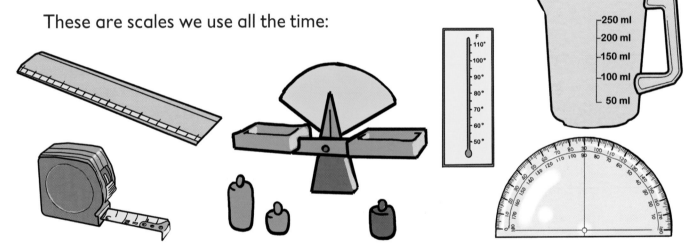

- The simplest scale you use is a ruler. A measuring tape is like a long ruler. Rulers and measuring tapes usually measure in centimetres and/or metres.

- We use weighing scales for measuring mass (how heavy something is) e.g. bathroom scales and kitchen scales. When we measure how heavy something is we use kilograms and grams. Your weighing scales probably show imperial units too (stones, pounds and ounces).

- The volume of a liquid is the amount of space it takes up. You might have measuring jugs, in the kitchen or garage, that are used to measure liquids like water, milk and oil. Volume is measured in millilitres and litres.

- A thermometer is used to measure temperature. The unit of measurement is a degree centigrade. We use the symbol ° C.

- A protractor is a tool we use to measure the degrees in an angle (you used one on page 11). The symbol is °.

Reading a Scale
Most of the time it can be easy to read a scale.

Sometimes, however, not all of the numbers are written on, and you have to work them out for yourself. In some case you have to estimate the reading.

The scale only shows volume in 50 ml amounts. You can see that the liquid is half way between 100 ml and 150 ml, so you know that there is approximately 125 ml of liquid.

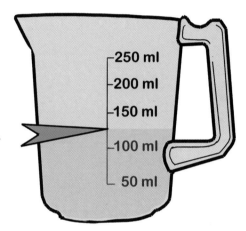

Home Learn

Read these scales:

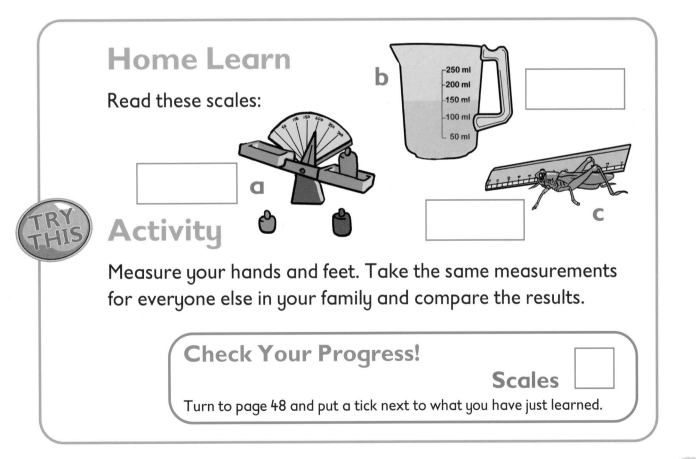

TRY THIS **Activity**

Measure your hands and feet. Take the same measurements for everyone else in your family and compare the results.

Check Your Progress!

Scales

Turn to page 48 and put a tick next to what you have just learned.

Parents Start Here...

Help your child to draw their own mealtime table for the family. Once it is completed you can help them draw some conclusions from the data. If you have a computer at home, you could generate a table and input the data together.

Top Tip! Learning is fun, so if your child is tired, let them come back to this when they are fresh.

Collecting Information

When we record information we write it down so we can remember it. Writing down information (or data) in a table makes it easier to understand.

Tally Marks

Bobby and Billy love playing table football. They are keeping a record of how many games they have each won. Every time Bobby wins a game he adds another mark below his name, and Billy does the same.

Billy	Bobby
ⱠⱠ	ⱠⱠ
ⱠⱠ	ⱠⱠ
‖	

These are tally marks. You write four lines then put the fifth across them. Then you can count in fives, which makes adding up the tally marks even easier. But even without counting, you can tell that Billy has won most games so far.

Tables

Claudia has three children and they always complain at mealtimes. So she drew up a big table and stuck it to the kitchen wall. Every time she cooks a meal she writes it on the table. Each child ticks the meals they are prepared to eat without moaning (too much!).

After one week the table looked like the one at the top of the opposite page.

	Abigail	Edmund	Sebastian
spaghetti bolognese	3		3
roast chicken	3	3	3
Chinese noodles and vegetables		3	
fish fingers and chips			3
pork chops and new potatoes	3	3	3
chicken casserole	3		
pasta and tuna	3	3	3

This table has been very useful for Claudia; she can see straight away which meals the children will all enjoy. It has also helped the children understand how difficult it is for their Mum to prepare a meal that pleases everyone!

Home Learn

Look at Claudia's table and answer these questions:

1. How many meals will each child eat without complaining:
   Abigail _____ Edmund _____ Sebastian _____

2. How many meals will all three children eat without complaining? _____

3. Which child is the most fussy? _____

Activity

Draw your own meal-time table like Claudia's and help everyone in your family to fill it in. Think about what you can learn from your table once it is complete.

Check Your Progress!
Collecting Information
Turn to page 48 and put a tick next to what you have just learned.

Top Tip!
If your child struggles with anything, don't worry – let them go at their own pace.

Parents Start Here...

Help your child conduct their own survey as suggested in the Activity. Supply graph paper to draw the bar chart, or you may have a programme on a home computer that would help with this part of the exercise.

Presenting Information: Bar Charts And Pie Charts

We have seen that putting data into tally marks and tables can be useful. There are other useful ways to present information too.

Bar Charts

Mrs Grimmer asked her pupils to choose their favourite subjects at school. She put the answers in to a table like the one shown here:

How many children did Mrs Grimmer talk to in her survey? _____

another word for total is frequency

Subject	Tally marks	Total
Maths	ＴＨＴ I	6
English	ＴＨＴ	5
P.E.	ＴＨＴ ＴＨＴ I	11
History	III	3
Science	ＴＨＴ I	6

Then she put her results into a bar chart like the one shown below:

A bar chart is another way of showing information. It can make looking at numbers more interesting. The results of the survey are certainly very easy to understand when you look at them this way.

Which was the most popular subject? _____

Turn this book on its side and look again at Mrs Grimmer's tally marks. Can you see that they make a pattern similar to the bar chart?

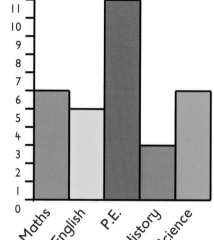

Number of children

Pie Charts

Pie Charts are based on a circle. Here is the information that Mrs Grimmer recorded, shown as a pie chart.

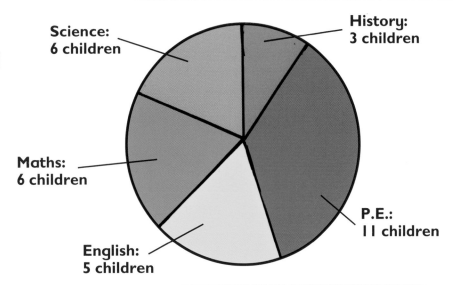

Science: 6 children

History: 3 children

Maths: 6 children

P.E.: 11 children

English: 5 children

Home Learn

Some children have recorded their classmates' favourite fruits. Complete the bar chart using the figures from this table:

apples	bananas	pears	cherries	peaches
‖‖‖	‖‖‖ ‖‖‖	‖‖‖	‖	‖‖‖ ‖‖
Totals				

Activity

Do a survey like Mrs Grimmer's one. Draw up a list of 5 television programmes and ask your friends to each pick their favourite. Record your data with tally marks, then ask a grown-up to help you put your results into a bar chart.

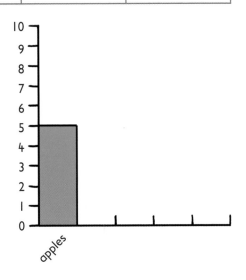

apples

Check Your Progress!
Bar Charts And Pie Charts

Turn to page 48 and put a tick next to what you have just learned.

Parents Start Here...

Weather charts in travel brochures are a good place to see both bar charts (for rain) and line graphs (for temperatures) put to practical use.

Presenting Information: Line Graphs

Line graphs are another way of showing information. They are similar to a bar graph but they are most often used when you are measuring time.

- A line graph has 2 axes, one along the bottom and one that goes up the side.

- The bottom axis is the one that normally has time on it.

One Tuesday during the school holidays, Jane counted how many times her son, Hugh, said 'I'm bored'. She recorded the 'I'm bored's and put them in a table like this:

	9–10 am	10–11 am	11–12 pm	12–1 pm	1–2 pm	2–3 pm	3–4 pm
	I	III	IIII	IIII III	IIII I	III	I
Frequency	1	3	5	8	6	3	1

Then Jane turned the table into a line graph, like this:

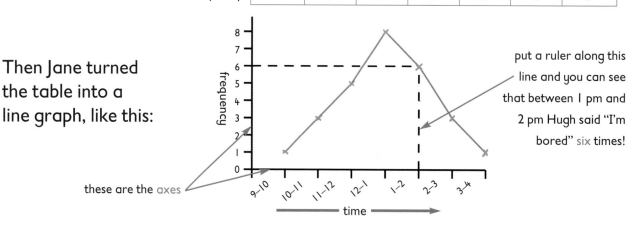

these are the axes

put a ruler along this line and you can see that between 1 pm and 2 pm Hugh said "I'm bored" six times!

The time is along the bottom and the frequency is up the side. Jane marked the frequency with crosses, and then she joined them all with a line.

Once Jane had drawn her line graph she could see that Hugh got most bored between 11 a.m. and 2.30 p.m. She decided to take him on a lunchtime picnic on Wednesday!

Try doing this line graph yourself.

Max is writing Christmas cards and putting them into envelopes. This table shows how many he has done:

Time (mins)	Cards
5	10
10	20
15	30
20	40
25	50

Now put the numbers on to the graph. Start with the first row of the table.

After 5 minutes Max had done 10 cards – so go along the bottom of the graph to find 5 minutes.

Look along the side of the graph to find 10. Imagine two lines drawn from these points – where they meet is where you put your cross.

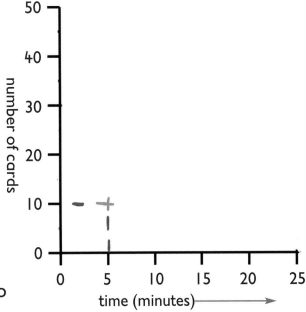

Carry on until you have got 5 crosses on the graph and you can draw a line to connect them all.

Home Learn

Look at your graph and answer these questions:
a) How many cards had Max done after 15 minutes?
b) Estimate how many cards Max had done after $22\frac{1}{2}$ minutes.
c) Estimate how many cards Max would have done after 30 minutes.

Activity

Look in a newspaper for any types of charts, tables or graphs. Now you understand something about how to present data, you should be able to work out what they are telling you.

Check Your Progress!
Line Graphs

Turn to page 48 and put a tick next to what you have just learned.

Activities

1. Look at this bar chart and complete the sentences:

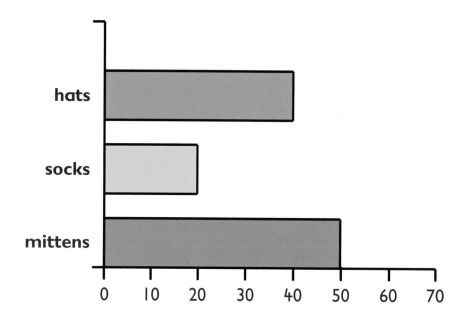

Clare knitted _____ hats, _____ mittens and _____ socks for the newborn babies.

2. This pie chart shows which types of fruit Form 5T took to school in their lunchboxes one day:

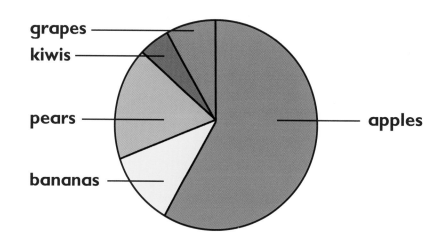

Which was the most popular fruit? _____

Which was the least popular fruit? _____

3. Use the data from the table to complete this line graph:

	JAN	FEB	MAR	APR	MAY	JUNE	JULY	AUG	SEPT	OCT	NOV	DEC
Rainfall in mm	6	5	5	14	29	30	38	37	31	27	19	12

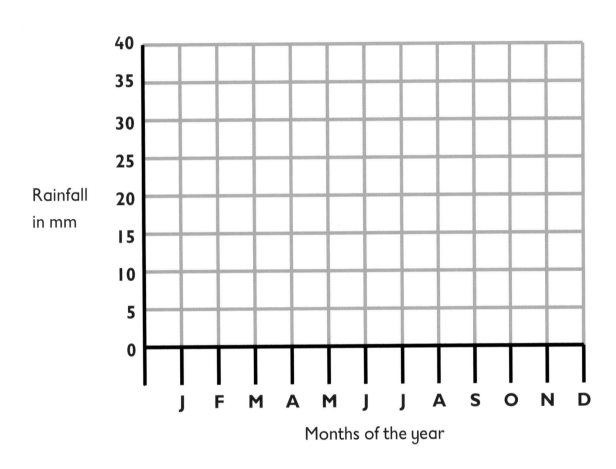

Rainfall in mm

Months of the year

Do you think these rainfall measurements were taken in the United Kingdom? Yes _____   No _____

Give the reasons for your answer:

_____

_____

Note: before you move onto the next page find a calculator; you will need one.

Top Tip!
Remember to give your child lots of praise – they'll work so much better.

Parents Start Here...

Calculators are permitted in part of the Key Stage Two Numeracy exams.

Using A Calculator

A calculator is a very handy tool if you learn how to use it properly. Some calculations could take ages if you are doing them in your head or on paper; using a calculator may save time. There are some things that are worth remembering, though.

- It is easy to press the wrong buttons!

- It is a good idea to have a rough estimate of the answer in your head before you begin. Then, if you make a mistake with the calculator, you will spot it.

- Calculators can not tell you about money or measurements, so you will still have to put the correct symbols into the answer.

Look at this picture of a calculator. The buttons on your calculator may be in different places. See if you can find all of the ones that are shown here.

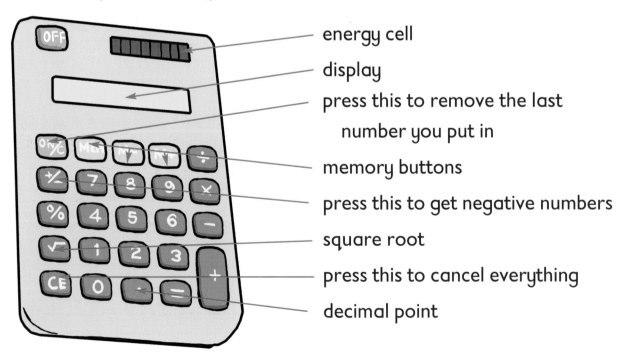

energy cell

display

press this to remove the last number you put in

memory buttons

press this to get negative numbers

square root

press this to cancel everything

decimal point

Try this calculation: 5 $\times$ 5 $=$ 25
Now press the square root button $\sqrt{}$. The displays shows 5.

Try this calculation: 4 $\times$ 4 $=$ 16. Press $\sqrt{}$.
Can you describe what the square root button is doing?

_____

What number is displayed if you press 1 0 0 followed by $\sqrt{}$? _____

Now experiment with the memory buttons (they are probably labelled with the letter M). See if you can work out what they all do.

Try these calculations on your calculator:

1205 x 3 = _____   4678 − 679 = _____
9633 ÷ 3 = _____   555 + 444 = _____

Now look at these calculations again. Could you have done any of them in your head?

Home Learn

Use your calculator to work this problem out, but remember to make a rough estimate first.

Tommy went into the shop and bought 18 packets of sausages for his barbecue. Each packet contained 12 sausages. There were 36 people at the barbecue and they shared the sausages equally. How many sausages did each person get? ☐

TRY THIS

Activity

Turn your calculator upside down and start putting some numbers in. You will find that some of the numbers now look like letters. See if you can make any words appear e.g. 637 upside down says 'leg'.

Check Your Progress!
Using A Calculator ☐
Turn to page 48 and put a tick next to what you have just learned.

Top Tip!
Don't worry if your child does not understand straightaway – children learn at different speeds.

Parents Start Here...

This is just an introduction to the subject of probability. It is a confusing subject, so it is worth taking it slowly and reinforcing with lots of practical experiments (use coins, cards and dice).

Probability

Probability means how likely something is to happen.

What is the probability of picking a black card from normal pack of playing cards? There are equal numbers of red and black cards in a pack, so there is an equal chance of picking a red or black card.
Look at that on the probability line.

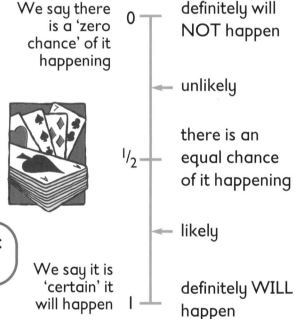

We say there is a 'zero chance' of it happening

0 — definitely will NOT happen

← unlikely

$\frac{1}{2}$ — there is an equal chance of it happening

← likely

We say it is 'certain' it will happen

1 — definitely WILL happen

We can say equal chance in different ways:
evens • I chance in 2 • 1 : 2

Look again at the probability line.

What is the probability of throwing a dice and getting a 7?
Point to the place on the line that matches your answer.

The answer is zero chance – you cannot throw a 7.

What is the probability of throwing an odd number?
Point to the place on the line that matches your answer.

You should be pointing at 'equal chance' ($\frac{1}{2}$) Why?
Because there are 6 possible numbers you could throw, and 3 of them, ($\frac{1}{2}$), are odd numbers.

You can test this. Get a dice and start throwing it. Each time you throw a number write it into this tally chart. After you have thrown your dice 40 times add up the totals.

1	
2	
3	
4	
5	
6	

How many times did you throw an even number? _____
How many times did you throw an odd number? _____

The two numbers in your answer boxes should be similar – not necessarily the same but quite close.

Half the time you threw an odd number, half the time you threw an even number.

With dice, cards and coins you can measure probability. You can not measure the probability of it raining tomorrow – but you can make a sensible judgement about it.

Jack and Julia can not decide on the likelihood of rain!

Who do you think has made the most sensible judgement?

> I think it will probably rain tomorrow because it has rained for the last few days, and the sky is full of heavy grey clouds

> I think it is likely that there won't be any rain tomorrow – we've had so much rain already there can't be any left!

Home Learn

When you throw a dice there is a one in six (1 : 6) chance of throwing a 5 because 5 is one of 6 possible numbers.
a) What is the chance of throwing a 1? _____
b) What is the chance of throwing a number higher than 3? _____

TRY THIS Activity

Look back at the tally chart you completed when you threw your dice 40 times. Did you get a similar frequency for each number? Try throwing the dice another 40 times and add the totals. Compare the frequencies now.

Check Your Progress!

Probability ☐

Turn to page 48 and put a tick next to what you have just learned.

Crossword

Clues Across

1. Every number up to 10 has one of these (5)
2. Short for litre (1)
3. There are 60 of these in one hour (6)
8. 3-D shape with a square base (7)
10. Width x _____ = area (6)
11. 3-D shape that's ideal for ice-cream (4)
12. There are _____ millimetres in a centimetre (3)
14. There are 24 hours in a _____ (3)
15. Same as 11 across
19. Temperature is measured in ° _____ (1)
20. Rotational, mirror and translation are all types of this (8)
21. A quadrilateral for a windy day (4)

Clues Down

1. If it's not an analogue clock it is _____ (7)
4. 3-sided polygon with angles that add up to 180° (8)
5. A measure of turn (5)
6. 3-D shape for kicking around (6)
7. There are 60 of these in a minute (6)
9. Length x width = _____ (4)
13. Short for metre (1)
16. Use a shape _____ to make a cube (3)
17. Short for kilometre (2)
18. Short for gram (1)

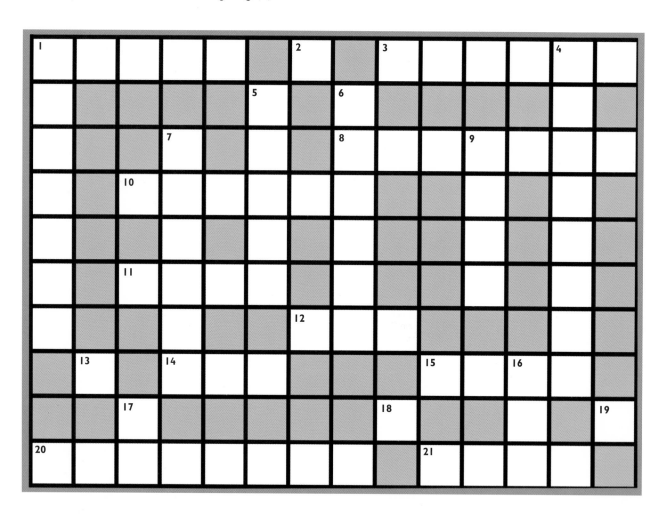

Answers

Page 5
Home Learn

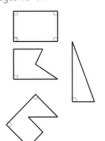

r

a

o

r

Page 7
Home Learn

a) A quadrilateral has 4 sides.
b) A triangle has 3 sides.
c) A pentagon has 5 sides.
d) A hexagon has 6 sides.
e) An octagon has 8 sides.

Page 9
Home Learn

3-D Shape	Corners	Edges	Faces
cube	8	12	6
cuboid	8	12	6
triangular prism	6	9	5
square based pyramid	5	8	5
regular tetrahedron	4	6	4

Page 11
Home Learn

a) 40°
b) 100°
c) 90°

Pages 12–13
Perimeter = 4 cm + 2 cm + 4 cm
+ 2 cm = 12 cm

Home Learn
You need to work out the unknown lengths
first:
8 cm – 6 cm = 2 cm
5 cm + 7 cm = 12 cm
Now you can add these lengths to the others
you were given:
8 cm + 5 cm + 6 cm + 7 cm + 2 cm + 12 cm
= 40 cm

Pages 14–15
Area: 3 x 4 cm = 12 cm²

Home Learn
Cut the shape into two squares, then work out
their areas:
3 cm x 3 cm = 9 cm²
2 cm x 2 cm = 4 cm²
Now add the totals: 9 cm² + 4 cm² = 13 cm²

Pages 16–17
Circus ring radius: 13 m

Home Learn
a) Approximately 300 cm
b) 50 cm

Pages 18–19

1.

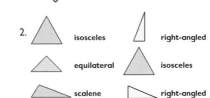

2.

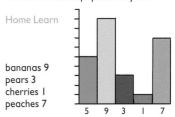

isosceles   right-angled

equilateral   isosceles

scalene   right-angled

4. a) 3 cm²
b) 10 cm²
c) 2 cm²

Page 21
Home Learn

Page 25
Home Learn
5 cm x 4 cm x 3 cm = 60 cm2

Page 27
Home Learn
Page 29

00:05	17:20
16:48	23:59
12:05	4:48

Home Learn
1. Train C
2. Train B
3. 26 minutes

Page 31
Home Learn
a) A pen is about 15 cm long.
b) An apple weighs about 100 g.
c) Most people are less than 2 m tall.
d) I can walk 6 km in one hour.

Page 33
Home Learn
a) 200 g
b) 150 ml
c) 80 mm/8 cm

Page 35
Home Learn
1. Abigail will eat 5 meals without complaining.
Edmund will eat 4 meals without complaining.
Sebastian will eat 5 meals without complaining.
2. There are 3 meals all the children will eat
without complaining.
3. Edmund is the fussiest child.

Pages 36–37
Bar charts:
Mrs Grimmer spoke to 31 children.
P.E. was the most popular subject.

Home Learn

bananas 9
pears 3
cherries 1
peaches 7

5 9 3 1 7

Page 39
Home Learn
a) 30 cards
b) Approximately 45 cards.
c) Approximately 60 cards.

Pages 40–41
1. Clare knitted 40 hats, 50 mittens and 20
socks for the newborn babies.
2. Apples were the most popular fruit.
Kiwis were the least popular fruit.
3.

Rainfall
in mm

J F M A M J J A S O N D
Months of the year

It is unlikely that these measurements were
taken in the UK because we usually get lots of
rain in the winter rather than the summer.

Page 43
1205 x 3 = 3615
4678 – 679 = 3999
9633 ÷ 3 = 3211
555 + 444 = 999

Home Learn
They got 6 sausages each:
18 x 12 = 216
216 ÷ 36 = 6

Page 45
Home Learn
a) 1 in 6
b) 3 out of 6 (or 1 out of 2).
There are three numbers higher than 3: 4, 5
and 6.

Page 46

Check Your Progress

Angles .... ☐

2-D Shapes .... ☐

3-D Shapes .... ☐

Triangles .... ☐

Measuring Perimeters .... ☐

Measuring Area .... ☐

Circles .... ☐

Symmetry .... ☐

Making 3-D Shapes .... ☐

Time .... ☐

Adding And Subtracting Time...................................... ☐

Measurements .... ☐

Scales .... ☐

Collecting Information .... ☐

Bar Charts And Pie Charts .... ☐

Line Graphs .... ☐

Using A Calculator .... ☐

Probability .... ☐